Cinebook recounts
The Wright Brothers

Written by: J.P. Lefevre-Garros
Illustrated by: Marcel Uderzo
Colour work: Monique Ott

9th CINEBOOK
The 9th Art Publisher

Original title: Les frères Wright

Original edition: © Editions du Lombard (Dargaud-Lombard SA) 2005
by M. Uderzo & J. P. Lefevre-Garros
www.lelombard.com

English translation: © 2008 Cinebook Ltd

Translator: Luke Spear
Lettering and text layout: Imadjinn sarl
Printed in Spain by Just Colour Graphic

This edition first published in Great Britain in 2011 by
Cinebook Ltd
56 Beech Avenue
Canterbury, Kent
CT4 7TA
www.cinebook.com

A CIP catalogue record for this book
is available from the British Library

ISBN 978-1-84918-100-6

9th CINEBOOK
The 9th Art Publisher

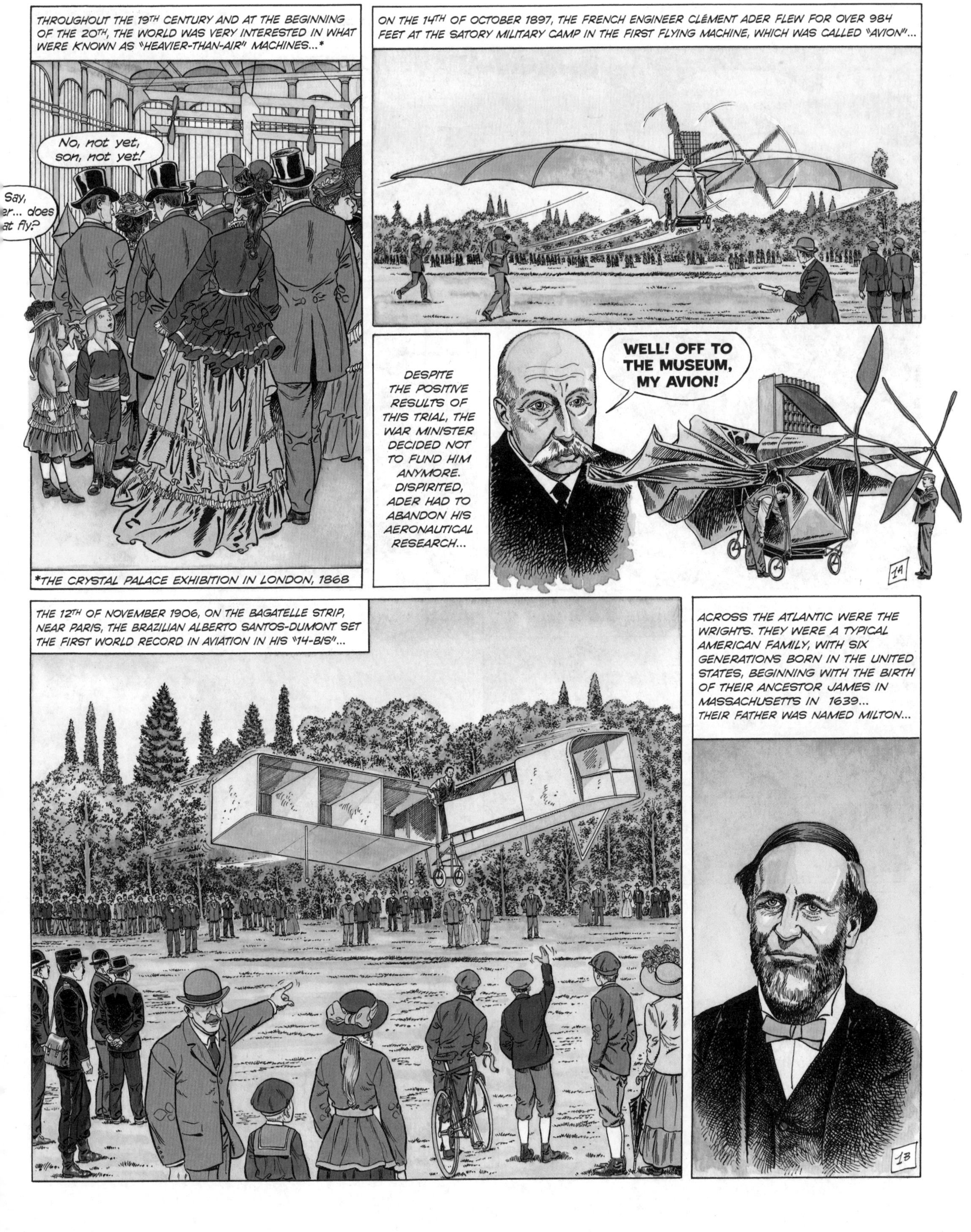
THROUGHOUT THE 19TH CENTURY AND AT THE BEGINNING OF THE 20TH, THE WORLD WAS VERY INTERESTED IN WHAT WERE KNOWN AS "HEAVIER-THAN-AIR" MACHINES...*
No, not yet, son, not yet!
Say, er... does at fly?
*THE CRYSTAL PALACE EXHIBITION IN LONDON, 1868
ON THE 14TH OF OCTOBER 1897, THE FRENCH ENGINEER CLÉMENT ADER FLEW FOR OVER 984 FEET AT THE SATORY MILITARY CAMP IN THE FIRST FLYING MACHINE, WHICH WAS CALLED "AVION"...
DESPITE THE POSITIVE RESULTS OF THIS TRIAL, THE WAR MINISTER DECIDED NOT TO FUND HIM ANYMORE. DISPIRITED, ADER HAD TO ABANDON HIS AERONAUTICAL RESEARCH...
WELL! OFF TO THE MUSEUM, MY AVION!
THE 12TH OF NOVEMBER 1906, ON THE BAGATELLE STRIP, NEAR PARIS, THE BRAZILIAN ALBERTO SANTOS-DUMONT SET THE FIRST WORLD RECORD IN AVIATION IN HIS "14-BIS"...
ACROSS THE ATLANTIC WERE THE WRIGHTS. THEY WERE A TYPICAL AMERICAN FAMILY, WITH SIX GENERATIONS BORN IN THE UNITED STATES, BEGINNING WITH THE BIRTH OF THEIR ANCESTOR JAMES IN MASSACHUSETTS IN 1639...
THEIR FATHER WAS NAMED MILTON...

MILTON WAS A BISHOP IN A BRANCH OF THE METHODIST CHURCH, THE UNITED BRETHREN IN CHRIST.

My dear brothers, let us pray that the Lord...

MARRIED TO SUZANNE, HE WAS A WARM AND LOVING SORT, ENCOURAGING HIS FIVE CHILDREN—FOUR BOYS AND A GIRL—TO STUDY, RAISING THEM WITH THE RIGOUR OF HIS OWN PRINCIPLES.

Dearest children, to succeed in life, you'll need to study, and study more... But beware of people... they are all ill-intentioned.

SUZANNE'S GRANDFATHER HAD EMIGRATED AT THE START OF THE 19TH CENTURY FROM HIS NATIVE SAXONY. JOHN GOTLIEB KOERNER SET UP AS A FARMER AND CARRIAGE MAKER...

FROM THEIR YOUTH, SUZANNE AND MILTON'S YOUNGEST SONS WILBUR AND ORVILLE REMAINED VERY CLOSE, SHARING THE SAME GAMES, THE SAME STUDIES, THE SAME PROJECTS...

Hey, Ullam*, do you think that one day, we too will be able to fly?

It was nice of Father to bring us this planophore... And it flies well!

*ULLAM: WILBUR'S NICKNAME

You know, Orv, I'm sure of it!

AFTER SEVERAL YEARS OF NOMADIC LIFE IMPOSED BY THE BISHOP'S MINISTRY, IN 1884 THE WRIGHT FAMILY SETTLED DOWN IN A LARGE WOODEN HOUSE AT 7 HAWTHORNE STREET IN DAYTON, OHIO.

IN 1889, SUZANNE KOERNER-WRIGHT PASSED AWAY AT THE AGE OF 59...

AS THE TWO OLDER BROTHERS WERE ALREADY MARRIED, ONLY MILTON, WILBUR, ORVILLE AND CATHERINE WERE LEFT IN THE HOUSE...

AND DESPITE BEING ONLY 15 YEARS OLD, YOUNG CATHERINE WOULD TAKE OVER HER MOTHER'S ROLE WHILE PURSUING HER STUDIES. FROM THAT POINT ON, FAMILY LIFE WOULD BE ORGANISED AROUND HER AT 7 HAWTHORNE STREET...

Orv, the time has come to start up our printing works...

DURING THIS "PRINTING" PERIOD, ORVILLE WOULD FURTHER DEVELOP HIS MECHANICAL SENSE AND EVEN INVENT A PRINTING PRESS THAT WOULD EARN HIM THE RESPECT OF PROFESSIONALS...

Look, Orv! Here's the text that we'll publish to defend Father's views against his church's reformers...

Ullam! This week's Dayton "West Side News" is ready!

BUT ALL THAT ACTIVITY DIDN'T EXTINGUISH THE PASSION THEY HAD FOR THE "HEAVIER-THAN-AIR" MACHINES...

Did you hear, Orv? Lilienthal's glider is... well, it flies, I tell you, it flies!

5

He has made hundreds of glides...

But how can he assure stability?...

Well, on that point I don't completely agree with him... You see... Lilienthal modifies the centre of gravity by moving his legs...

Whereas you'd advocate wing warping...

Yes, which would change the shape of certain elements of the frame... A sort of wing-warping!

Say, Orv! I thought that we might appoint a manager now for the printers and set up our bicycle workshop... What do you think?

All right, big brother...

FROM 1892, IN THEIR NEW WORKSHOP AT 1127 WEST SIDE STREET, THEIR INTEREST IN ALL THINGS MECHANICAL WOULD DEVELOP. THEY SOON REACHED A HIGH LEVEL OF SKILL...

WHILE WORKING AT THE SHOP, WILBUR CONTINUED TO DEVOUR EVERYTHING PUBLISHED ON MECHANICAL FLIGHT...

WILBUR EVEN WENT AS FAR AS WRITING TO THE SMITHSONIAN INSTITUTION TO GET FURTHER EXPLANATIONS AND A LIST OF BOOKS DEALING WITH THE SUBJECT...

IN 1896...

GOODNESS GRACIOUS, ORV! LILIENTHAL!...

What about Lilienthal?

A crash! He's just gotten himself killed!... He'd already made over 2000 glides...

Fortunately, he's left us his work and calculation tables! They'll be useful...

We have to start by constructing a kite that will allow us to study the effects of flight surfaces on stability... No more than 5 feet in wingspan...

Yes, and I can see a device like Chanute's, the one that Herring flew at Dune Park... A small biplane in trellis structure with a horizontal rudder at the rear...

Like on the Penaud planophore...

Without forgetting the ballast centre of gravity...

IN 1899, NOT FAR FROM THEIR HOME...

... THE EXPERIMENT CARRIED OUT BY THE TWO BROTHERS PROVED TO THEM THE SUPERIORITY OF WING WARPING OVER OTHER METHODS OF STABILISATION USED BEFORE...

You see, Orv! We were right! The buzzard maintains its lateral balance thanks to the curve in the edges of its wings!

... WILBUR FINALLY DECIDED TO WRITE TO OCTAVE CHANUTE TO SHARE THEIR EXPERIMENTS AND PROJECTS...

7

AT THIS TIME, THE FRENCH-AMERICAN OCTAVE CHANUTE WAS NOT ONLY A RECOGNISED AND REPUTED THEORETICIAN OF THE HEAVIER-THAN-AIR, BUT HE HAD ALREADY DESIGNED AND BUILT SEVERAL MACHINES...

No... This one looks serious!

... I am afflicted with the belief that flight is possible for man...

Another one who thinks he's got it!

And my disease will soon cost me plenty of money, if not my life...

... Due to our professional obligations, we can only devote the months of September to January to our experiments...

This boy understands how it all works!...

IN HIS LETTER, WILBUR NOTED THAT IN FIVE YEARS, LILIENTHAL HAD ONLY FLOWN A TOTAL OF 5 HOURS...

... For me, practice is more necessary than machinery...

And what's more, he's right, the old chap!

To acquire this practice, one has to be able to fly for many hours in complete security.

IN ORDER TO DO THIS, WILBUR CAME UP WITH AN EXTRAORDINARY SYSTEM COMPOSED OF A TOWER 115 FEET HIGH WITH THE SUMMIT ATTACHED TO THE GLIDER BY A BEAM AND A ROPE...

He mustn't use that mast. It's far too dangerous!

OH, NO! HE'S GONE COMPLETELY OFF THE TRACKS THERE!

The first attempts must be made over sand—softer on landing...

... As for places that I deem interesting for your attempts, they would be California and Florida...

WITH HIS REPLY, CHANUTE INCLUDED THE REPORT OF HIS OWN FLIGHT EXPERIMENTS... AND THEN...

... And then a book by Frenchman Mouillard on experimental safety, thinking it would be useful to him...

9

IN AUGUST 1900...

If I believe Lilienthal's and our own calculations, to support a man in a wind of 16mph you'd need a surface area of 150 square feet...

FROM THEIR DISCUSSIONS AND CALCULATIONS, A SMALL BIPLANE NAMED "CANARD" WAS FINALLY BORN. A LITTLE OVER 16 FEET IN WINGSPAN AND A TOTAL AREA OF ABOUT 161 SQUARE FEET ...

... And the pilot will be laid out in a cradle 18 inches wide on the lower wing in order to reduce wind resistance...

FOR THE WING PROFILE, THEY ADOPTED A CURVATURE WITH A PEAK THAT WASN'T LOCATED IN THE CENTRE (AS IN LILIENTHAL'S AND CHANUTE'S DESIGNS) BUT NEARER THE LEADING EDGE OF THE WING...

That gives us a ratio of 1/24 instead of 1/12 for the others...

Empty, the whole thing weighs only 49 pounds!

And will only have cost 15 dollars!...

Let's face it: Florida and California are really too far! Have you news from North Carolina?

Yes! I got a reply from the Kitty Hawk postmaster... It's a fishing village located on the coastal spit... We've found what we're looking for there...

Yes... sand and wind!

ON THE 6TH OF SEPTEMBER 1900, WILBUR WENT ON AHEAD AND LEFT DAYTON FOR KITTY HAWK...

At least six days to reach Kitty Hawk...

IN THE NORFOLK PORT...

LESS THAN TWO DAYS LATER...

CAREFUL! IT'S FRAGILE!

Are you Israel Perry?

Yes, I received your mail, Mr Wright. Ready to leave for Kitty hawk, once we've boarded your equipment.

I bought this pine and ash in Norfolk. I wasn't going to burden myself from Dayton with all that!

BILL TATE, THE POSTMASTER HE'D WRITTEN TO, WELCOMED HIM INTO HIS HOME WHILE AWAITING THE ARRIVAL OF ORVILLE, WHO HAD THE CAMPING GEAR.

Kitty-Hawk. N.C. Post Office

... BUT WILBUR REMAINED OBSERVANT AND ACTIVE...

The buzzard maintains balance with difficulty in bad weather, with its wings at a dihedral angle when gusts of cross-wind trouble it, while the falcon and the eagle, which keep their wings in normal positions, easily maintain their balance.

HE BORROWED HIS HOST'S MECHANICAL SAW TO ADVANCE THE CONSTRUCTION OF THE FIRST GLIDER...

11

ORVILLE DIDN'T TAKE LONG TO JOIN HIM, LEAVING CATHERINE TO LOOK AFTER THE "WRIGHT CYCLE CO"...

Orders, deliveries, accounts... You'll manage very well...

Of course! I never doubted it!

AT KITTY HAWK, ORVILLE BROUGHT THE TENT AND THE NECESSARY EQUIPMENT FOR THEIR CAMPAIGN OF 1900...

You know, Wilbur, trying to camp around here constantly reminds me of the Arctic explorers...

Oh, you're exaggerating a little... But this northeasterly wind is truly glacial!

THEIR DAILY LIFE WAS NO MORE ENVIABLE: THEY HAD NO FUEL FOR FIRE, SO NOT EVEN ANY HOT DRINKS...

On today's menu: this morning, biscuits with tomatoes in conserve and eggs! Tonight, eggs and tomatoes in conserve, with biscuits!...

... But with dessert, a spoonful of condensed milk...

THEIR SPARTAN LIFE DIDN'T STOP THEM FROM CONTINUING CONSTRUCTION OF THE FIRST GLIDER...

AND SOON...

FOR THE FIRST TRIAL OF WHAT THEY NOW CALLED THE MACHINE, THE TWO BROTHERS BORROWED A LOADING MAST FROM THE VILLAGE...

Orv! Are the 50 pounds of chains well fastened?

Yes, I've centred the ballast where we said...

UNFORTUNATELY, THE MACHINE WAS RIPPED DOWN BY THE WIND AND SLIGHTLY DAMAGED. THIS PROCEDURE WAS IMMEDIATELY ABANDONED...

It's nothing! We'll soon have it repaired...

THE 17TH OF SEPTEMBER, THEY TRANSPORTED THE CRAFT A MILE AWAY FROM CAMP...

Lucky that we made it light!

We'll try it as a kite first, just with the ballast!...

TAKING TURNS, THE TWO BROTHERS TOOK THEIR PLACES AS PILOT...

And you, Tom, do you want to try as well?

Oh, yes, Mr Wright...

THE 18TH, THE WIND WASN'T STRONG ENOUGH TO CARRY THE PILOT, BUT THEY TRIED, ANYWAY, AND FOUND A GOOD METHOD FOR TAKEOFF...

Hold the machine until it's supported by the air, and then run down the slope!

13

Well, well! It's easy to control the altitude...

And the wing warping acts the same as for the kite...

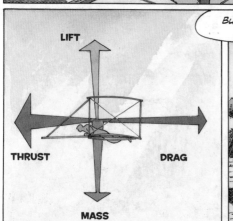

LIFT

THRUST

DRAG

MASS

But the lift is still too weak...

Could we have been mistaken in our calculations?

DOUBTS BEGAN TO TAKE HOLD OF THEM...

Or how about the tables we used: are they reliable?

This year, we'll make a few more flights, use the glider as a kite to take measurements of drag and lift, and then we'll stop until next year.

We'll come back with another glider!

THIS FIRST CAMPAIGN AT KITTY HAWK ALLOWED THEM TO CEMENT THEIR IDEAS OF FLIGHT CONTROL: THEY LEARNT THE TAKEOFF METHOD, THE PILOT'S POSITION OF LYING ON THE STOMACH, TURNED OUT TO BE COMFORTABLE AND DANGER-FREE... ON THEIR RETURN TO DAYTON, ON THE 16TH OF NOVEMBER 1900, WILBUR WROTE TO CHANUTE...

We have spent a great deal of our time measuring thrust and drag in winds of differing speeds and with varying loads... The distances covered have varied between 200 and 400 feet at an angle of 1/6 (10°) and the landing speed was over double that of takeoff, the wind blowing at around 12 miles an hour. We had no difficulty keeping longitudinal balance...

STILL BUSY WITH HIS MULTIPLE OCCUPATIONS, CHANUTE WAS ONLY FINALLY ABLE TO MEET THE WRIGHT BROTHERS ON THE 26TH OF JUNE 1901 AT THEIR DAYTON HOME...

I brought this anemometer from my last trip to Paris. You can use it on your glider.

Thank you very much, Mr Chanute. This new glider is larger than the last... 22 feet instead of 16 feet in wingspan...

Giving 291 square feet instead of 161 square feet...

I see... This way you will obtain more lift...

Wing curvature is now 1/12, but we can modify that over the trials.

How will you do that?

Look! We've built small masts and a whole system of cables to modify it.

Interesting!

As for me, I have continued construction of my latest gliders! I intend to have them tested by my assistant Huffaker...

IT WAS ALMOST AS THOUGH THE MASTER WAS NOW SEEKING ADVICE FROM HIS STUDENTS...

Well, we will be starting work in Kitty Hawk on the 7th of July. Why not couple the trials of your gliders with ours?

Not this year, but next year. And then we can compare our results...

15

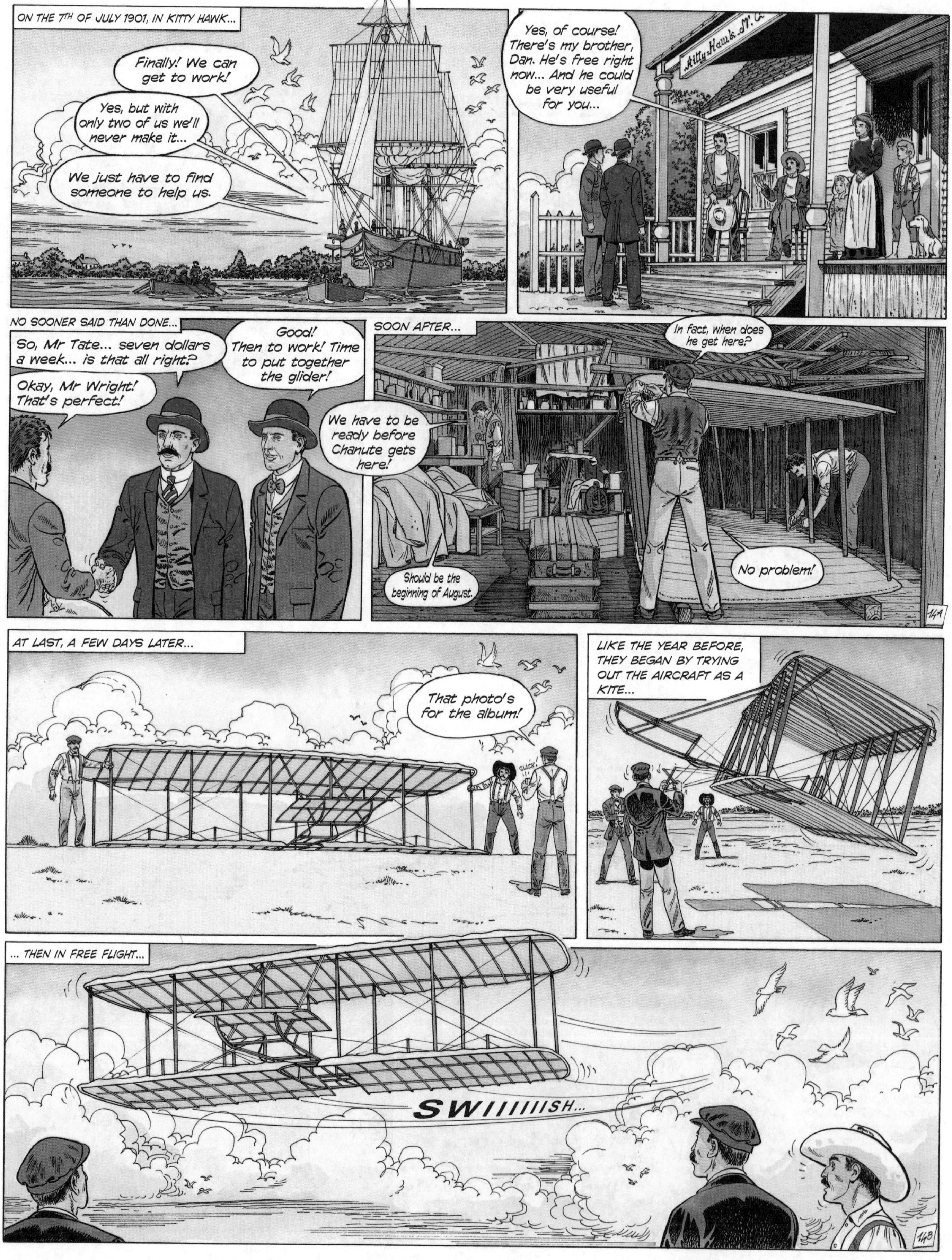
ON THE 7TH OF JULY 1901, IN KITTY HAWK...
Finally! We can get to work!
Yes, but with only two of us we'll never make it...
We just have to find someone to help us.
Yes, of course! There's my brother, Dan. He's free right now... And he could be very useful for you...
NO SOONER SAID THAN DONE...
So, Mr Tate... seven dollars a week... is that all right?
Okay, Mr Wright! That's perfect!
Good! Then to work! Time to put together the glider!
SOON AFTER...
In fact, when does he get here?
We have to be ready before Chanute gets here!
Should be the beginning of August.
No problem!
AT LAST, A FEW DAYS LATER...
That photo's for the album!
CLICK!
LIKE THE YEAR BEFORE, THEY BEGAN BY TRYING OUT THE AIRCRAFT AS A KITE...
... THEN IN FREE FLIGHT...
SWIIIIIIISH...

... THEN WILBUR FINALLY PUT HIMSELF AT THE CONTROLS...

Right, Dan. First we'll run, then we have to let go...

Okay, Mr Orville...

Strange—feels like the altitude control is softer than in the old one...

SWIIIIIISH

SWIIIIIISH...

SOME 17 FREE GLIDING FLIGHTS FROM JULY TO AUGUST RAISED THE ENTHUSIASM OF THE FEW SPECTATORS PRESENT...

BRAVO! BRAVO!

WOOF WOOF!

THE 8TH OF AUGUST...

The wind is at 12mph!

367 feet in 12 and a half seconds! Our record for 1901!

Heh heh! Chanute was right when he said the prone position could be dangerous!

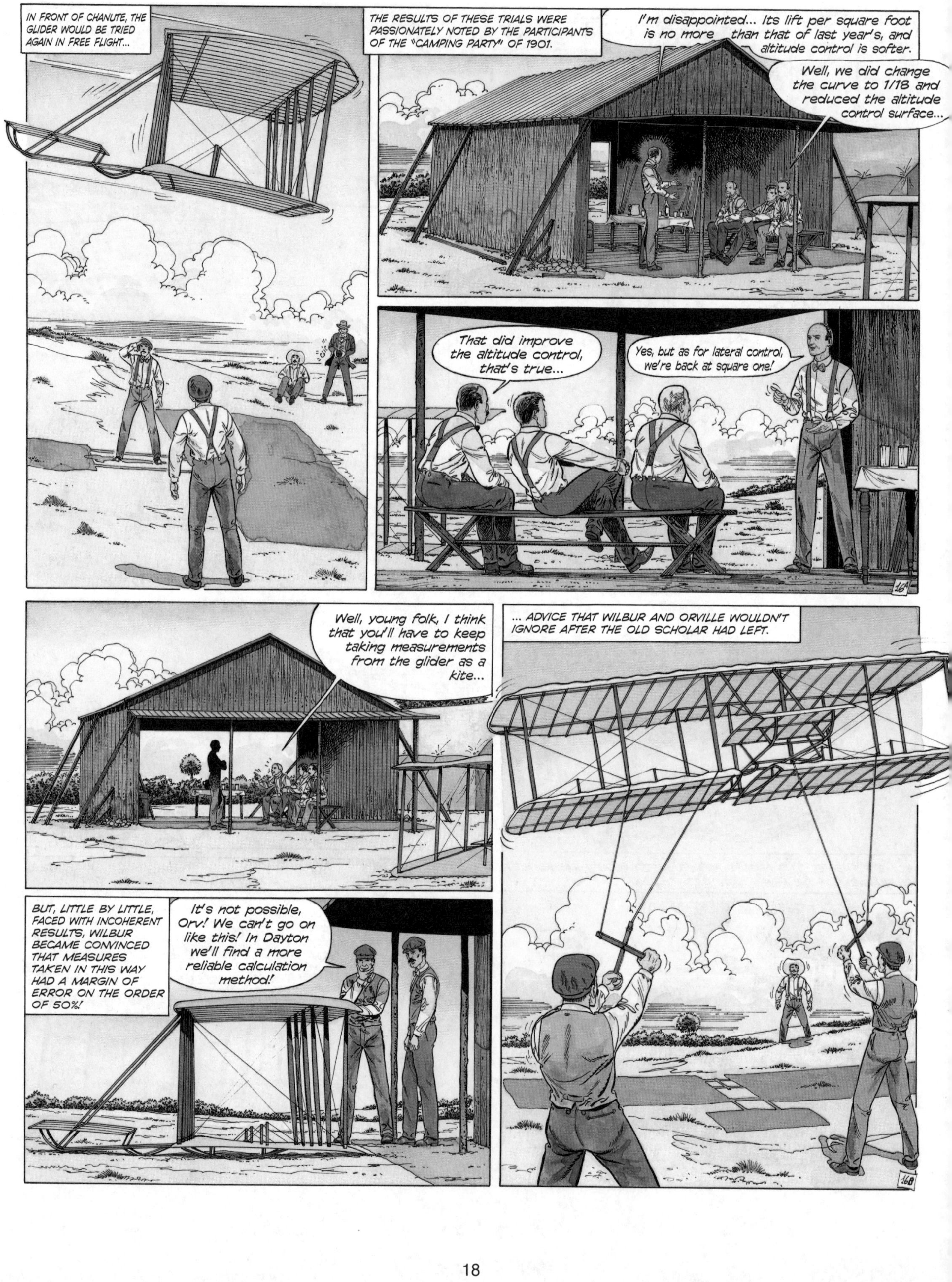
IN FRONT OF CHANUTE, THE GLIDER WOULD BE TRIED AGAIN IN FREE FLIGHT...
THE RESULTS OF THESE TRIALS WERE PASSIONATELY NOTED BY THE PARTICIPANTS OF THE "CAMPING PARTY" OF 1901.
I'm disappointed... Its lift per square foot is no more than that of last year's, and altitude control is softer.
Well, we did change the curve to 1/18 and reduced the altitude control surface...
That did improve the altitude control, that's true...
Yes, but as for lateral control, we're back at square one!
16A
Well, young folk, I think that you'll have to keep taking measurements from the glider as a kite...
... ADVICE THAT WILBUR AND ORVILLE WOULDN'T IGNORE AFTER THE OLD SCHOLAR HAD LEFT.
BUT, LITTLE BY LITTLE, FACED WITH INCOHERENT RESULTS, WILBUR BECAME CONVINCED THAT MEASURES TAKEN IN THIS WAY HAD A MARGIN OF ERROR ON THE ORDER OF 50%!
It's not possible, Orv! We can't go on like this! In Dayton we'll find a more reliable calculation method!
16B

THE 18TH OF SEPTEMBER 1901, WILBUR WAS IN CHICAGO, GIVING A CONFERENCE ON THE STATE OF THEIR TRIALS...

The birth of the aeroplane is near, and we can already say... gentlemen... that all the basic problems are resolved...

WESTERN SOCIETY OF ENGINEERS

... And that those remaining—propeller, motor, etc.—will be a lot easier to resolve...

THIS FINE OPTIMISM WAS A LITTLE PREMATURE, AS THEY STILL NEEDED TO DETERMINE THE IDEAL WING PROFILE... BY ANY MEANS POSSIBLE...

No, that won't do it!

THEY EVEN INSTALLED A "LABORATORY" ON A CYCLE...

I don't think I can do two things at once!...

What we need to study our wing profiles, Orv, is a fixed machine that provides us with wind at a predetermined speed.

AND SO, ONE OF THE FIRST WIND TUNNELS IN THE WORLD WAS CREATED...

With a wind of 30mph, we'll be able to calculate our own drag and lift coefficients.

THEY THUS PROCEEDED TO STUDY 200 WING PROFILES...

BROOOUUUB

You see, Ullam, a longer wing is better than a short and wide wing!...

SATISFIED WITH THE RESULTS OF THEIR OBSERVATIONS, THEY COULD NOW GET STARTED ON THE CREATION OF THEIR NEW AIRCRAFT, BASED ON MORE SOLID FOUNDATIONS...

Well, Orv, for it to fly better, our 1902 glider must have a longer wingspan...

Yes, and 10 more feet of wingspan will only add an extra 11 square feet...

Okay for the lift, but how to counter the effects of wing warping?

You mean, for the control of the third axis...

Yes, that's really troubled us this year.

Well, we could try to fix a rudder to the back.

A rudder? Why not?

IT WAS ALMOST INSTINCTIVELY THAT THE WRIGHT BROTHERS ADDED A RUDDER TO THEIR GLIDER IN 1902...

OVER THE EVOLUTION OF THE "MACHINE," THIS RUDDER WOULD FIRST BE DOUBLE AND FIXED, THEN SINGLE AND LINKED TO WING WARPING CONTROLS, AND FINALLY CONTROLLABLE, WHICH BECAME THE UNIVERSAL SOLUTION...

IN THE YEAR OF GRACE 1902, AT KITTY HAWK, THE END OF AUGUST...

At last! We're back!

You know, winter has been quite tough, Mr Wilbur!

I can see that! We'll just have to put the barn back in a fit state...

And in order to work in there, we'll need to get the 1901 glider out first. That'll give us more room.

Oh, great! The wind's picking up!

THE WRIGHT BROTHERS AND DAN TATE WERE REPAIRING THE WINTER DAMAGES, WHEN, ALL OF A SUDDEN, WITH A LOUD CRASH, A GUST FLIPPED THE 1901 GLIDER OVER, BREAKING PART OF THE FRAME...

?!

CRAAACK!...

FORTUNATELY, THE WOOD NEEDED TO BUILD THE NEW GLIDER HAD BEEN BOUGHT ON THE WAY...

Never mind. We'll leave this one!

Come on, we can do this! We've brought all the wood here with us! Now, let's get to building the new glider!

AFTER ALL THESE INCIDENTS, IT WASN'T UNTIL THE 8TH OF SEPTEMBER THAT THEY COULD REALLY BEGIN BUILDING THE 1902 GLIDER...

... IT WOULD BE BUILT ENTIRELY ON SITE...

TWO DAYS LATER, IT WAS DIFFICULT FOR THE TWO BROTHERS TO RESIST...

Ullam! We could try the upper part right away, seeing as it's ready!

OK, Orv!

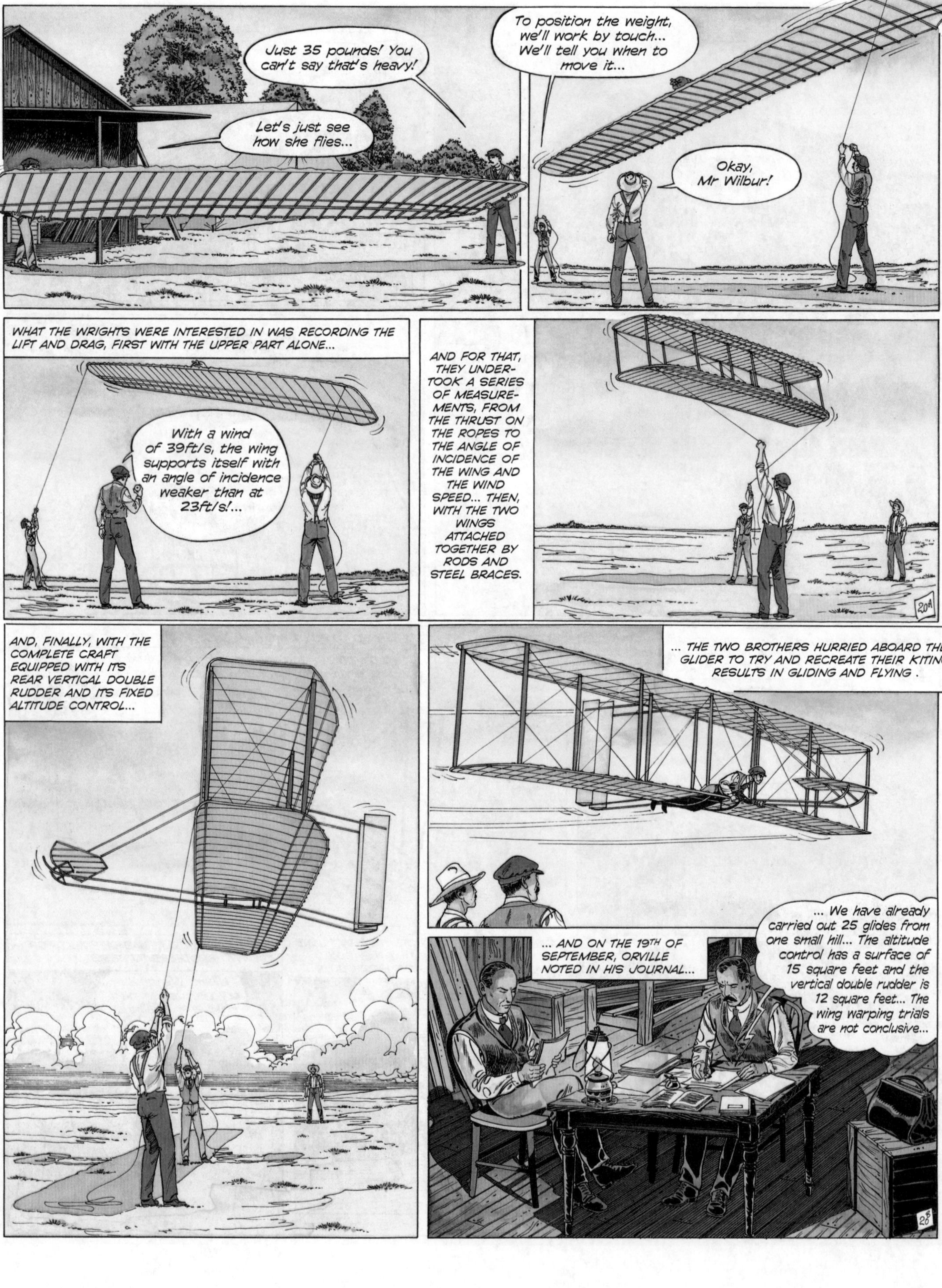
Just 35 pounds! You can't say that's heavy!
Let's just see how she flies...
To position the weight, we'll work by touch... We'll tell you when to move it...
Okay, Mr Wilbur!
WHAT THE WRIGHTS WERE INTERESTED IN WAS RECORDING THE LIFT AND DRAG, FIRST WITH THE UPPER PART ALONE...
With a wind of 39ft/s, the wing supports itself with an angle of incidence weaker than at 23ft/s!...
AND FOR THAT, THEY UNDERTOOK A SERIES OF MEASUREMENTS, FROM THE THRUST ON THE ROPES TO THE ANGLE OF INCIDENCE OF THE WING AND THE WIND SPEED... THEN, WITH THE TWO WINGS ATTACHED TOGETHER BY RODS AND STEEL BRACES.
20A
AND, FINALLY, WITH THE COMPLETE CRAFT EQUIPPED WITH ITS REAR VERTICAL DOUBLE RUDDER AND ITS FIXED ALTITUDE CONTROL...
... THE TWO BROTHERS HURRIED ABOARD THEIR GLIDER TO TRY AND RECREATE THEIR KITING RESULTS IN GLIDING AND FLYING .
... AND ON THE 19TH OF SEPTEMBER, ORVILLE NOTED IN HIS JOURNAL...
... We have already carried out 25 glides from one small hill... The altitude control has a surface of 15 square feet and the vertical double rudder is 12 square feet... The wing warping trials are not conclusive...
20B

MEANWHILE, THE WRIGHTS WERE ABLE TO MEASURE THE HEIGHT OF THE SURROUNDING DUNES... AND FROM THEN ON, IT WAS FROM THESE HILLS AT KILL DEVIL, HIGHER UP BUT QUITE FAR FROM THE CAMP, THAT THEY WOULD CONTINUE THEIR TRIALS...

SOON, THE TWO BROTHERS NOTICED THE SUPERIORITY OF THEIR NEW MACHINE...

This one can take off on a slope of 7 degrees!...

Whereas the old one needed at least 15!

WA-HOO!...

ON THE 20TH OF SEPTEMBER, WILBUR TESTED OUT WING WARPING, BUT...

Good gracious! Now it even glides on the right!

WILBUR MANAGED TO REDUCE THE LATERAL TILT A LITTLE...

... BUT ON LANDING...

!

CRAAAAKC!...

FORTUNATELY, THERE WAS NO SERIOUS DAMAGE...

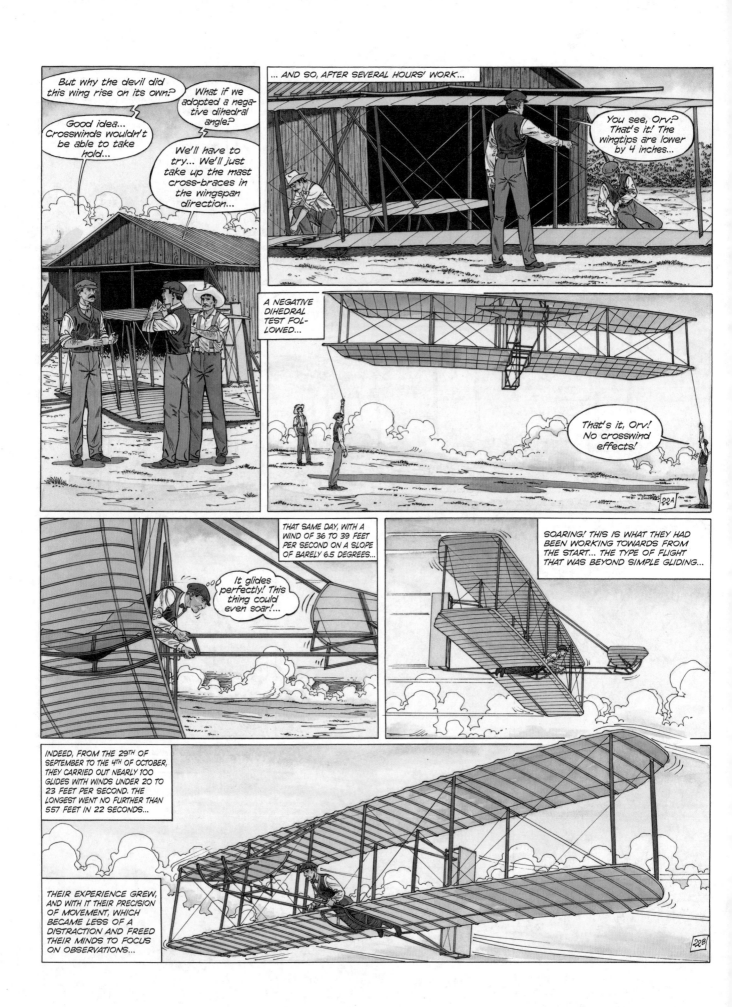

But why the devil did this wing rise on its own?

Good idea... Crosswinds wouldn't be able to take hold...

What if we adopted a negative dihedral angle?

We'll have to try... We'll just take up the mast cross-braces in the wingspan direction...

... AND SO, AFTER SEVERAL HOURS' WORK...

You see, Orv? That's it! The wingtips are lower by 4 inches...

A NEGATIVE DIHEDRAL TEST FOLLOWED...

That's it, Orv! No crosswind effects!

That same day, with a wind of 36 to 39 feet per second on a slope of barely 6.5 degrees...

It glides perfectly! This thing could even soar!...

SOARING! THIS IS WHAT THEY HAD BEEN WORKING TOWARDS FROM THE START... THE TYPE OF FLIGHT THAT WAS BEYOND SIMPLE GLIDING...

INDEED, FROM THE 29TH OF SEPTEMBER TO THE 4TH OF OCTOBER, THEY CARRIED OUT NEARLY 100 GLIDES WITH WINDS UNDER 20 TO 23 FEET PER SECOND. THE LONGEST WENT NO FURTHER THAN 557 FEET IN 22 SECONDS...

THEIR EXPERIENCE GREW, AND WITH IT THEIR PRECISION OF MOVEMENT, WHICH BECAME LESS OF A DISTRACTION AND FREED THEIR MINDS TO FOCUS ON OBSERVATIONS...

ON THE 5TH OF OCTOBER, WILBUR AND ORVILLE WELCOMED THEIR GUESTS...

My friend Herring*. Spratt will be along later. They want to try my two new craft! At my age, I can't do a great deal...

Oh, Mr Chanute!

*IN 1896, AUGUSTUS MOORE HERRING HAD HELPED HIS FRIEND CHANUTE BUILD THE BIPLANE GLIDER THAT HE HIMSELF TESTED.

Well, let's hope the weather's good. We'll carry out our own tests at the same time.

BUT NEITHER CHANUTE'S MULTIPLANE NOR HIS BIPLANE WITH MOVEABLE WINGS COULD MANAGE TO TAKE OFF...

ON THE OTHER HAND, THE WRIGHT GLIDER...

... WORKED ON BY THEIR OLDER BROTHER LORIN, WHO HAD COME TO LEND A HAND...

MARVELLOUS! A GLIDER IN MID TURN!

OVER THE COURSE OF HIS FRUITLESS TRIALS, CHANUTE HAD TO ADMIT HIS FAILURE...

OK, OK! I must conclude that my craft are unfit for flight...

VERY DISAPPOINTED, CHANUTE AND HERRING TOOK THEIR LEAVE ON THE 14TH OF OCTOBER AND LEFT THEIR CRAFT AT THE SITE...

My friends, I have to let you know that I'm going to be away for at least four months...

Oh, yes?

I'm taking the boat in January with my daughters, headed for Europe!

We've acquired some good experience and we can venture out in any weather!...

THAT NIGHT, THE TWO BROTHERS IN THEIR "LIVING ROOM"...

Wintering here is over for 1902! All that's left to think about now is our engine!

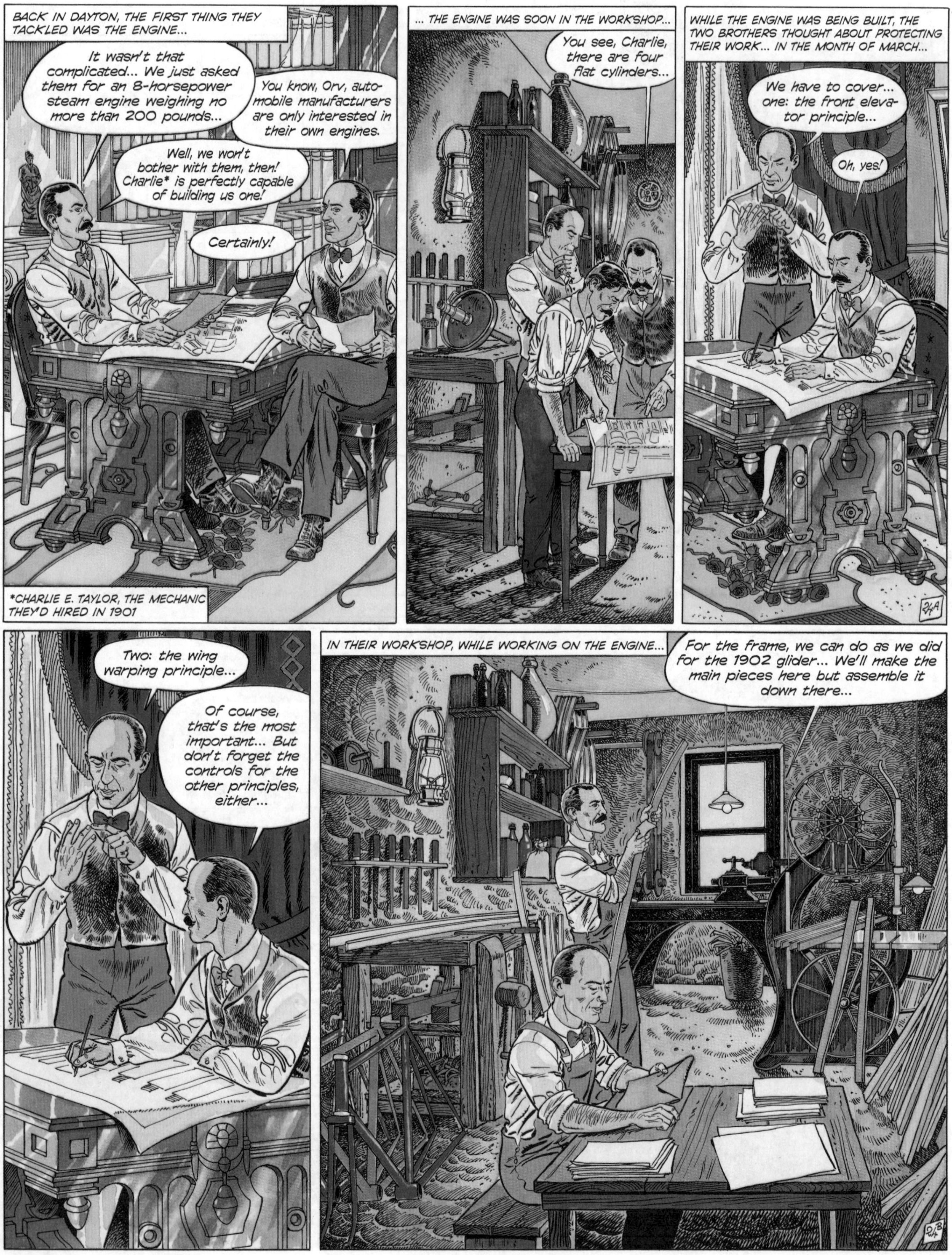
BACK IN DAYTON, THE FIRST THING THEY TACKLED WAS THE ENGINE...
It wasn't that complicated... We just asked them for an 8-horsepower steam engine weighing no more than 200 pounds...
You know, Orv, automobile manufacturers are only interested in their own engines.
Well, we won't bother with them, then! Charlie* is perfectly capable of building us one!
Certainly!
*CHARLIE E. TAYLOR, THE MECHANIC THEY'D HIRED IN 1901
... THE ENGINE WAS SOON IN THE WORKSHOP...
You see, Charlie, there are four flat cylinders...
WHILE THE ENGINE WAS BEING BUILT, THE TWO BROTHERS THOUGHT ABOUT PROTECTING THEIR WORK... IN THE MONTH OF MARCH...
We have to cover... one: the front elevator principle...
Oh, yes!
Two: the wing warping principle...
Of course, that's the most important... But don't forget the controls for the other principles, either...
IN THEIR WORKSHOP, WHILE WORKING ON THE ENGINE...
For the frame, we can do as we did for the 1902 glider... We'll make the main pieces here but assemble it down there...

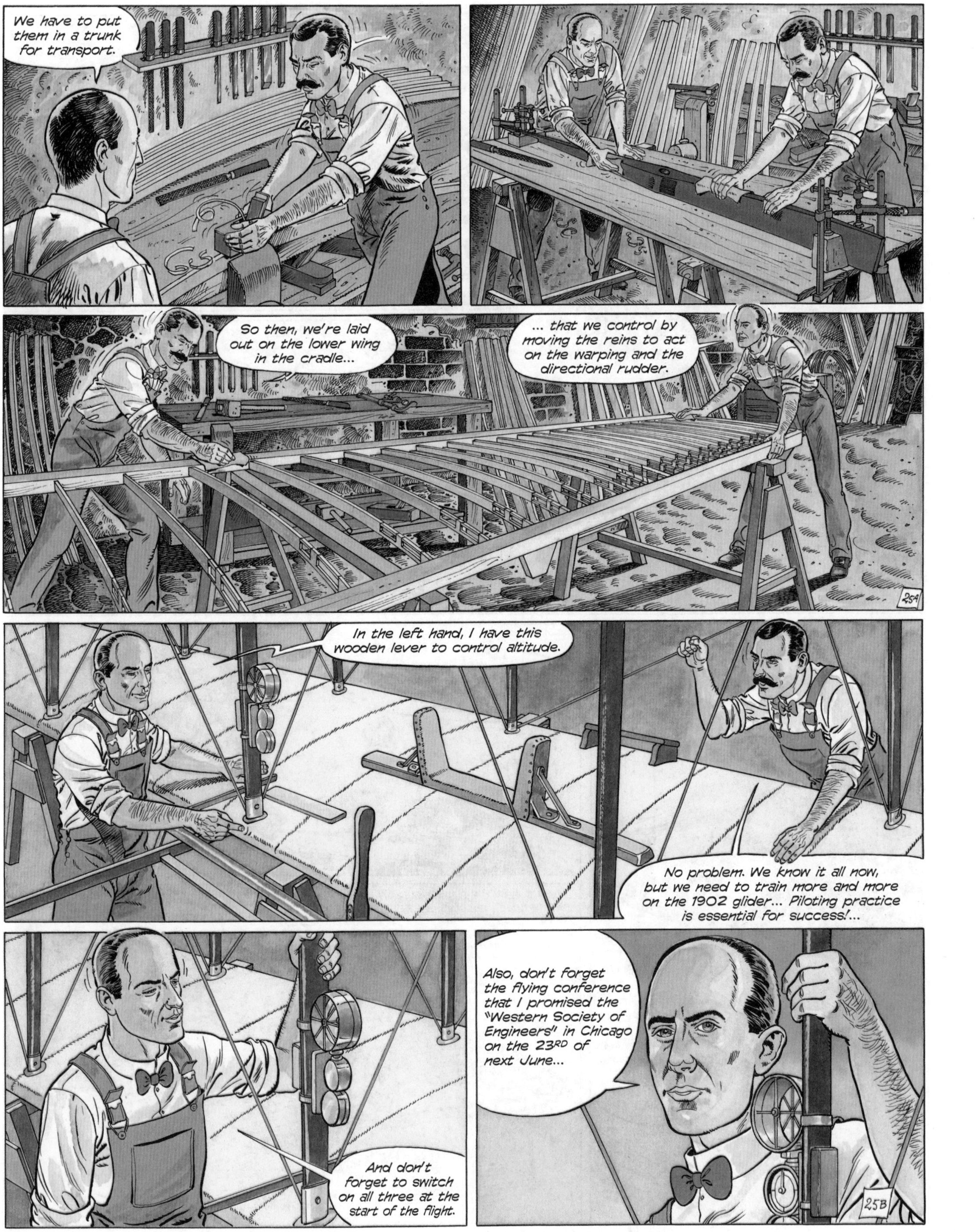
We have to put them in a trunk for transport.
So then, we're laid out on the lower wing in the cradle...
... that we control by moving the reins to act on the warping and the directional rudder.
25A
In the left hand, I have this wooden lever to control altitude.
No problem. We know it all now, but we need to train more and more on the 1902 glider... Piloting practice is essential for success!...
And don't forget to switch on all three at the start of the flight.
Also, don't forget the flying conference that I promised the "Western Society of Engineers" in Chicago on the 23RD of next June...
25B

ALL THESE PREPARATIONS CONSIDERABLY DELAYED THE TWO BROTHERS. IT WAS THE 23RD OF SEPTEMBER BEFORE THEY ARRIVED, IN 1903, AT THE EXPERIMENT SITE...

HELLO, SURFMEN!*

HELLO, FLYING MEN!

U.S. LIFE SAVING STATION

*LIFEGUARDS FOR THE FEDERAL LIFE SAVING SERVICE

Mr Daniels, I'm happy to see you... This year, the craft will be a lot heavier: it has an engine now...

An engine?

Yes, that's 200 pounds more to transport. We'll need your muscles...

Of course, that's okay.

And I thought, when we need you, we'd raise a red flag on the mast.

Okay! As soon as we see it, we'll come running!

BUT BEFORE GOING TO WORK ASSEMBLING THE CRAFT, THEY HAD TO BUILD IT A HANGAR FIRST...

Depending on the weather, we'll alternate between work on the ground and flights in the 1902 glider.

You're right, Orv! We haven't flown since last year and we have to practice our piloting before trying the engine...

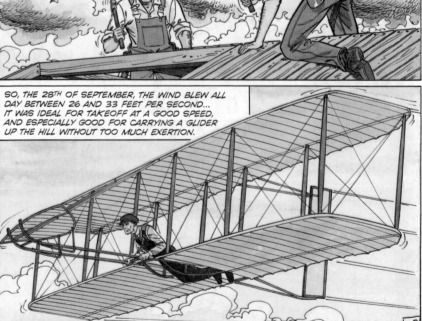

... And with longer flights on the glider, we can find some useful improvements for the machine!...

SO, THE 28TH OF SEPTEMBER, THE WIND BLEW ALL DAY BETWEEN 26 AND 33 FEET PER SECOND... IT WAS IDEAL FOR TAKEOFF AT A GOOD SPEED, AND ESPECIALLY GOOD FOR CARRYING A GLIDER UP THE HILL WITHOUT TOO MUCH EXERTION.

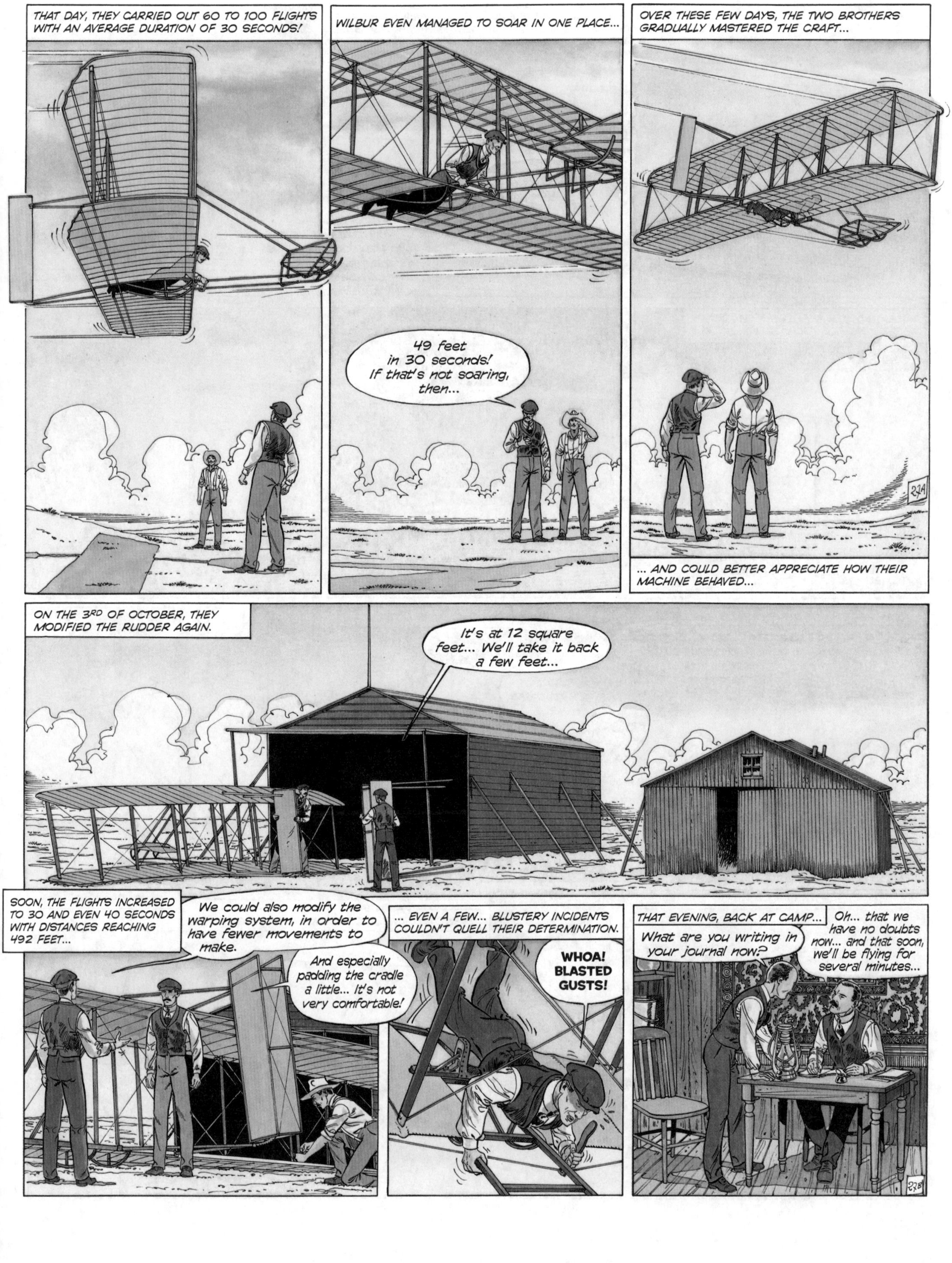

THAT DAY, THEY CARRIED OUT 60 TO 100 FLIGHTS WITH AN AVERAGE DURATION OF 30 SECONDS!
WILBUR EVEN MANAGED TO SOAR IN ONE PLACE...
49 feet in 30 seconds! If that's not soaring, then...
OVER THESE FEW DAYS, THE TWO BROTHERS GRADUALLY MASTERED THE CRAFT...
... AND COULD BETTER APPRECIATE HOW THEIR MACHINE BEHAVED...
ON THE 3RD OF OCTOBER, THEY MODIFIED THE RUDDER AGAIN.
It's at 12 square feet... We'll take it back a few feet...
SOON, THE FLIGHTS INCREASED TO 30 AND EVEN 40 SECONDS WITH DISTANCES REACHING 492 FEET...
We could also modify the warping system, in order to have fewer movements to make.
And especially padding the cradle a little... It's not very comfortable!
... EVEN A FEW... BLUSTERY INCIDENTS COULDN'T QUELL THEIR DETERMINATION.
WHOA! BLASTED GUSTS!
THAT EVENING, BACK AT CAMP...
What are you writing in your journal now?
Oh... that we have no doubts now... and that soon, we'll be flying for several minutes...

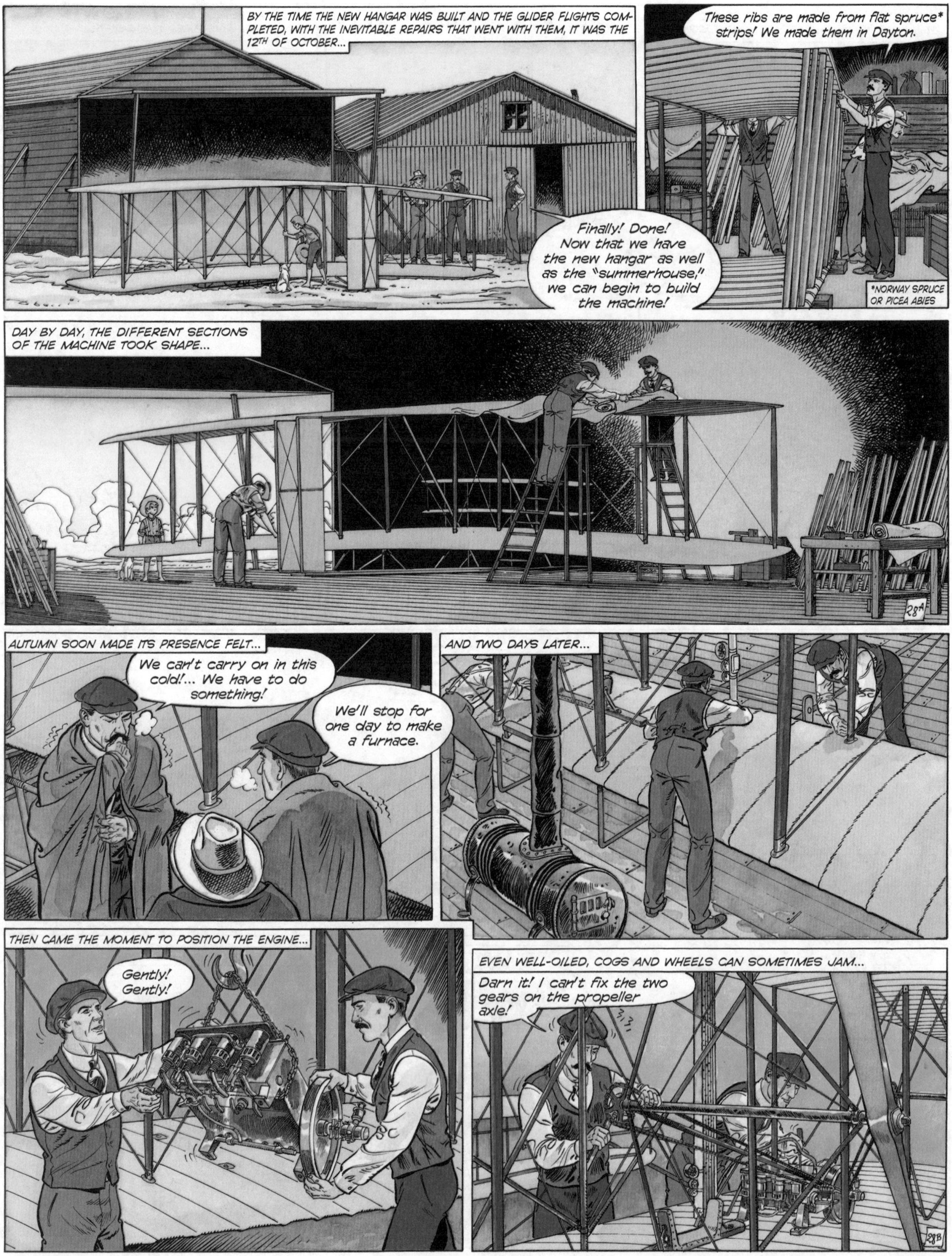
BY THE TIME THE NEW HANGAR WAS BUILT AND THE GLIDER FLIGHTS COMPLETED, WITH THE INEVITABLE REPAIRS THAT WENT WITH THEM, IT WAS THE 12TH OF OCTOBER...
Finally! Done! Now that we have the new hangar as well as the "summerhouse," we can begin to build the machine!
These ribs are made from flat spruce* strips! We made them in Dayton.
*NORWAY SPRUCE OR PICEA ABIES
DAY BY DAY, THE DIFFERENT SECTIONS OF THE MACHINE TOOK SHAPE...
28A
AUTUMN SOON MADE ITS PRESENCE FELT...
We can't carry on in this cold!... We have to do something!
We'll stop for one day to make a furnace.
AND TWO DAYS LATER...
THEN CAME THE MOMENT TO POSITION THE ENGINE...
Gently! Gently!
EVEN WELL-OILED, COGS AND WHEELS CAN SOMETIMES JAM...
Darn it! I can't fix the two gears on the propeller axle!
28B

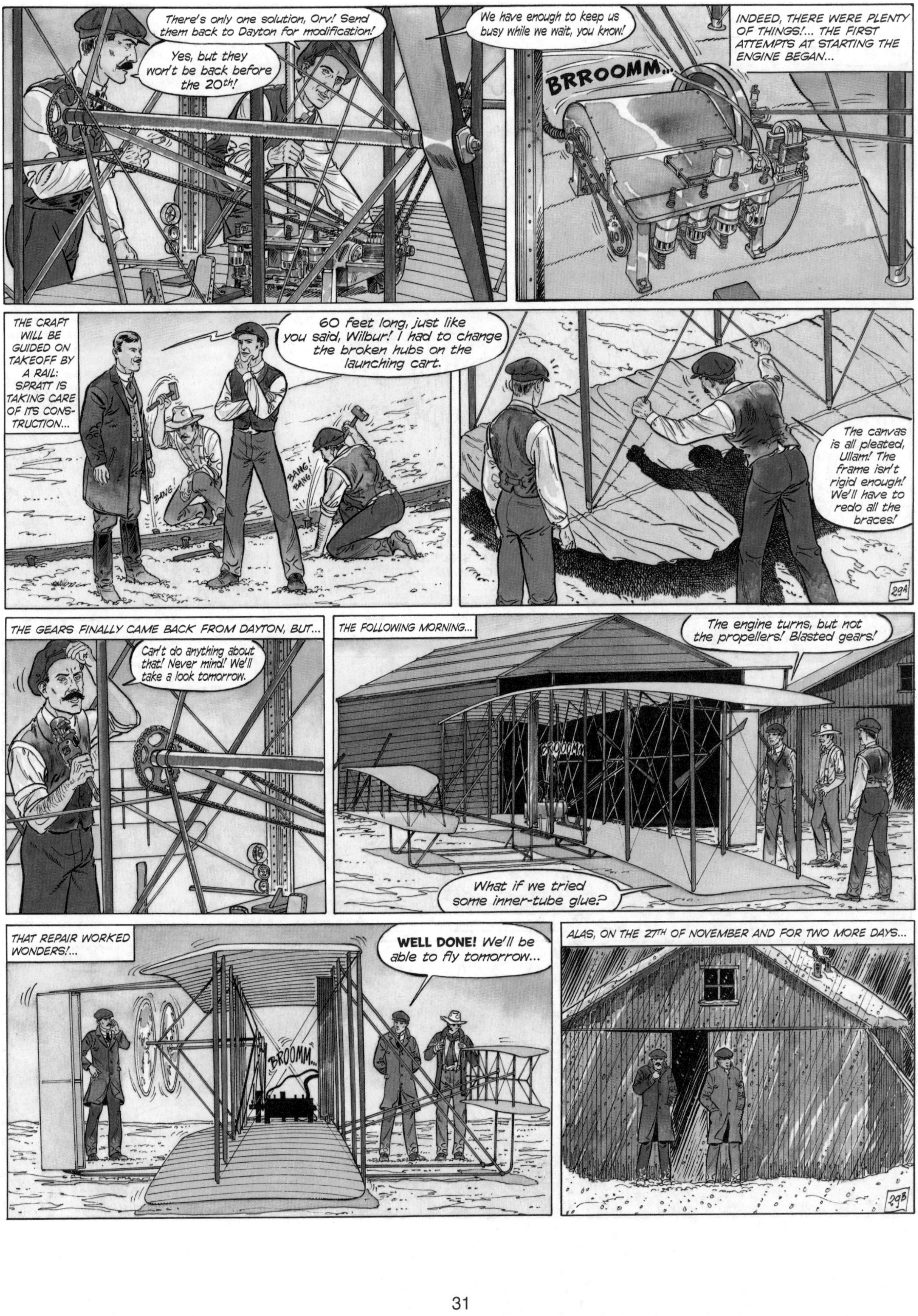
There's only one solution, Orv! Send them back to Dayton for modification!
Yes, but they won't be back before the 20th!
We have enough to keep us busy while we wait, you know!
INDEED, THERE WERE PLENTY OF THINGS!... THE FIRST ATTEMPTS AT STARTING THE ENGINE BEGAN...
BRROOMM...
THE CRAFT WILL BE GUIDED ON TAKEOFF BY A RAIL: SPRATT IS TAKING CARE OF ITS CONSTRUCTION...
60 feet long, just like you said, Wilbur! I had to change the broken hubs on the launching cart.
BANG!
BANG! BANG!
The canvas is all pleated, Ullam! The frame isn't rigid enough! We'll have to redo all the braces!
29A
THE GEARS FINALLY CAME BACK FROM DAYTON, BUT...
Can't do anything about that! Never mind! We'll take a look tomorrow.
THE FOLLOWING MORNING...
The engine turns, but not the propellers! Blasted gears!
BROOMM
What if we tried some inner-tube glue?
THAT REPAIR WORKED WONDERS!...
WELL DONE! We'll be able to fly tomorrow...
BROOMM...
ALAS, ON THE 27TH OF NOVEMBER AND FOR TWO MORE DAYS...
29B

EVEN THOUGH IT WAS STILL VERY COLD, CLEAR WEATHER CAME ANYWAY, AND SO, ON THE 28TH OF NOVEMBER...

THERE IT IS! *They've hoisted the red flag! They need us! Let's go!*

BROOM!... PUFF! PUFF! PAFF!

CUT THE ENGINE, ORV! IT'S GOING TO BLOW!

INDEED...

Nothing for it! The axle is cracked!

No more time to lose, Orv! This time, you leave immediately. We need more resistant axles as quickly as possible!

ORVILLE LEFT FOR DAYTON STRAIGHTAWAY, WHERE HE HAD NEW AXLES MADE.

You see, little sister, thanks to the glider, we learnt to pilot well. As soon as we have our new axles, there should be no more difficulties flying this motorized aircraft! Practice! That's what our predecessors lacked!

ON THE 11TH OF DECEMBER, ORVILLE COULD FINALLY MAKE HIS WAY BACK WITH THE PRECIOUS PROPELLER AXLES, AND ON THE TRAIN...

8TH OF DECEMBER FAILURE OF SECOND MECHANICAL FLIGHT ATTEMPT BY LANGLEY

*SAMUEL PIERPONT LANGLEY (1834-1906) WAS THE MAIN RIVAL OF THE WRIGHT BROTHERS.

... His craft "Aerodrome" dropped into the Potomac just after having been launched by a catapult installed on a real floating house, which cost the sum of...

50,000 DOLLARS FOR HIS FLOATING HOUSE! *That Langley is mad! Our launch rail cost us only 18 dollars!*

?!

?!

8TH OF DECEMBER FAILURES OF SECOND MECHANICAL FLIGHT ATTEMPT BY LANGLEY

THE 12TH OF DECEMBER, A SATURDAY...

"THE FLYER," CARRIED BY THE MEN, WAS PLACED ON THE RAIL ALONG THE "BIG KILL DEVIL HILLS" SLOPE...

Not a breeze! No way can we fly today...

We can at least try the takeoff procedure.

AND THEY HAD TO SATISFY THEMSELVES WITH MEASURING THE SPEED OF THE CRAFT ON ITS RAIL...

The last 15 feet in 1.5 seconds! That's 10.28mph! It's just not enough!

It isn't! The glider's flight speed was in the order of 25mph!

THE RAIL MEASURED 59 FEET IN TOTAL.

TO TOP IT ALL OFF, ON THE LAST ATTEMPT...

Not too much damage, luckily! It's over for today! We'll put the machine back in the hangar.

All right, we'll take another look on Monday...

FOR BISHOP MILTON WRIGHT'S SON, SUNDAY WAS A HOLY DAY. ONE DIDN'T WORK ON THE LORD'S DAY! BUT ONE MIGHT DISCUSS AND REFLECT...

Can you believe it, Orv! We're already nearly at mid-December.

And we haven't completed the upgrade yet!

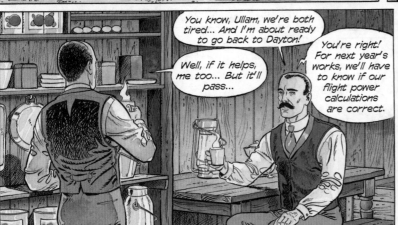

You know, Ullam, we're both tired... And I'm about ready to go back to Dayton!

Well, if it helps, me too... But it'll pass...

You're right! For next year's works, we'll have to know if our flight power calculations are correct.

THEIR HESITATION DIDN'T LAST FOR LONG...

Right! From tomorrow, Monday, or whenever the first favourable day is, we'll attempt a takeoff!

OK, big brother.

33

THE 14TH OF DECEMBER IN THE MORNING, AFTER THE TRADITIONAL FASTIDIOUS PREPARATIONS...

She'll be able to compensate for the weak wind!

I've marked out a slope over there of at least 8 degrees 50 minutes!

Tails! You start, lucky devil!

I CAN'T RELEASE THE RESTRAINING WIRE! COME AND HELP ME!

ETHERIDGE*! WHAT ARE YOU DOING? NOT HERE!... THERE!

RIGHT! AND WHAT SHOULD I DO NOW?

THAT'S IT! THE BOLT IS RELEASED!

*THE THREE SURFMEN WERE CALLED JOHN T. DANIELS, W.S. DOUGH AND A.D. ETHERIDGE. ALSO PRESENT WERE W.C. BRINKLEY FROM MANTEO AND JOHNNY MOORE FROM NAGS HEAD.

IN THE CONFUSION, THE PLANE LEFT THE RAIL 6 OR 10 FEET FROM THE END...

BUT WILBUR DIDN'T YET KNOW HOW EFFICIENT THE ALTITUDE CONTROL WAS... AND INEVITABLY...

... THE LANDING WASN'T DAMAGE-FREE!

115 feet... in 3.3 seconds!... But it's damaged!

AFTER A DAY AND A HALF OF REPAIRS, THE TRIALS WERE CALLED OFF DUE TO A LACK OF WIND...

No need to wear ourselves out—not a hint of a breeze! We'll try again tomorrow!

FORTUNATELY, THE FOLLOWING MORNING...

Not bad! 20.50 mph!

Yes, but this northerly wind is glacial! We have to raise the red flag to ask our friends to come help us.

With this wind, we could take off on flat land. Not too far from here. It's now or never!

AT 10.30AM ON THE 17TH OF DECEMBER, 1903, THE FLYER WAS PLACED ON THE RAMP... ORVILLE WAS AT THE CONTROLS...

AT 10.35AM...

FLYER 1 FLEW!...
IT WAS JOHN DANIELS WHO IMMORTALIZED THE SCENE ON ORVILLE'S CAMERA...

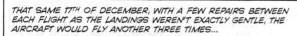

THAT SAME 17TH OF DECEMBER, WITH A FEW REPAIRS BETWEEN EACH FLIGHT AS THE LANDINGS WEREN'T EXACTLY GENTLE, THE AIRCRAFT WOULD FLY ANOTHER THREE TIMES...

It's your turn, Ullam!

It definitely seems like the altitude controls need checking!

164 feet in around 12 seconds!

OH! A gust has tipped it to the left!

The warping is OK. I managed to correct it without trouble!

197 feet in 15 seconds!

I think the altitude is too sensitive... The control stick is poorly placed...

I'll look into it!

ON THE THIRD FLIGHT OF THE DAY, WILBUR MANAGED 853 FEET IN 59 SECONDS!

IT WAS FROM THIS DAY ONWARD THAT THE WRIGHTS WOULD CALL THIS AND THEIR FOLLOWING MOTORIZED AIRCRAFT **"FLYER"**...

THE FLYER 1 WOULD NOT GROW OLD, THOUGH... DESPITE DESPERATE EFFORTS FROM DANIELS, THE CRAFT WAS OVERTURNED BY A BRUTAL GUST OF WIND AND BROKEN FOR GOOD...

GOOD HEAVENS! THIS THING IS GOING TO TURN ME OVER!!!

?!

CRACK...

THAT NIGHT, ORVILLE SUMMED UP THE DAY IN A TELEGRAPH TO HIS FATHER.

Success STOP! Four flights Thursday morning, all against a wind of 21 mph STOP! Take off solely powered by the engine at mid speed in the air, 31 mph STOP! Longer flight, 57 seconds, STOP! Inform press STOP! We'll be back for Christmas! Orville Wright

RATHER EXCITED BY THE FLYER'S SUCCESS, THE TWO BROTHERS NOW DECIDED TO UNVEIL THEIR EXPERIMENTS TO THE PRESS, AND, BACK IN DAYTON...

Well, you can publish all the results that we've given you.

And say, too, that we've worked alone.

And when can we photograph the craft?

Oh, no! No! No photos! No photos!

All right, gentlemen, I'll let the Associated Press know!

WHEN HE LEARNT OF THIS DECLARATION, CHANUTE WAS DEEPLY TROUBLED, AND HIS LETTER ON THE 14TH OF JANUARY WAS IN A RATHER BITTER TONE...

Worked alone! Worked alone? And what about me? They've gone too far, these young folk!

BUT THIS BITTERNESS SOON PASSED, AND IN HIS LETTER ON THE 29TH OF MARCH, 1904, WILBUR MADE NO ALLUSION TO THAT NOTE WHEN HE WROTE:

We're about to begin our new machine...

IT WAS ONLY AFTER THE FIRST FOUR SUCCESSFUL FLIGHTS THAT THE TWO BROTHERS NOTICED A MYRIAD OF PROBLEMS STILL TO RESOLVE...

CHANUTE ALSO SOON FORGOT THE INCIDENT, AND ON THE 14TH OF APRIL...

It's Chanute! He's announcing the creation of a prize in France: the Deutsch-Archdeacon Prize!*

*THE DEUTSCH-ARCHDEACON PRIZE OF 50,000 FRANCS FOR THE FIRST KILOMETRE OF A CLOSED CIRCUIT

DURING ITS FLIGHT ON THE 17TH OF DECEMBER, THE FLYER 1 HAD ONLY MAINTAINED A SIMPLE, STRAIGHT LINE. WITH THEIR NEXT AIRCRAFT, THE TWO BROTHERS WANTED TO BE ABLE TO CONTROL ITS DIRECTION, AS WITH THEIR 1902 GLIDER... SO IN THE MONTH OF APRIL 1904...

We'll keep the same engine model. But we'll push it to 16 horsepower...

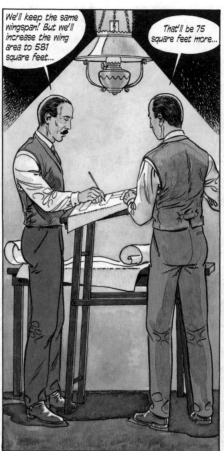

We'll keep the same wingspan! But we'll increase the wing area to 581 square feet...

That'll be 75 square feet more...

And for the length, we'll go from 22 feet to 28!

Yes, but we'll keep the propellers and the same general setup.

POWER PLANT

THEY STRIVED TO CORRECT THE MAIN DEFECTS THEY'D DETECTED IN THE FIRST MODEL...

We absolutely have to eliminate this wavy flight.

And modify the altitude control! It's too sensitive.

Easy! We just have to move the control axle further forward!

AND AS THE TRIPS TO AND FROM NORTH CAROLINA HAD LOST THEM ENOUGH TIME AND CAUSED PLENTY OF FATIGUE...

Of course! His land is useless to him!

You think it'll work?

The land is an old marsh that has become a pasture... 100 acres... Around eight miles from here... It's bordered to the west and north by trees.

The Springfield road is to the west, and to the south you have the electric tramway line.

That doesn't bother us... We're interested in it...

What we would like is your authorization to build a hangar on site, in order to manufacture and store our machine.

That's completely fine, gentlemen, completely!

AND FROM THE MONTH OF APRIL, 1904...

Before each trial, we'll have to clear all this livestock.

AFTER A SHORT WHILE, THE CONSTRUCTION OF FLYER II BEGAN.

If we want to keep it secret until the meeting with the journalists, we shouldn't fly while the tramway's passing.

Yes, it comes by every half hour.

Here there's no slope, next to no wind, but flat land... We'll have to seriously lengthen the rail...

Oh, yes, at least up to 200 feet.

BROOOOM...

FROM THE 20TH OF MAY, THE ENGINE AND PROPELLER TRIALS WERE SATISFACTORY; THEY INVITED THE PRESS FOR THE FOLLOWING WEEK...

Yes! The Wright brothers! You know the bicycle merchants from West Third Street... They say that they're going to be flying by the 23rd of May...

In Dayton? I'd like to see that!

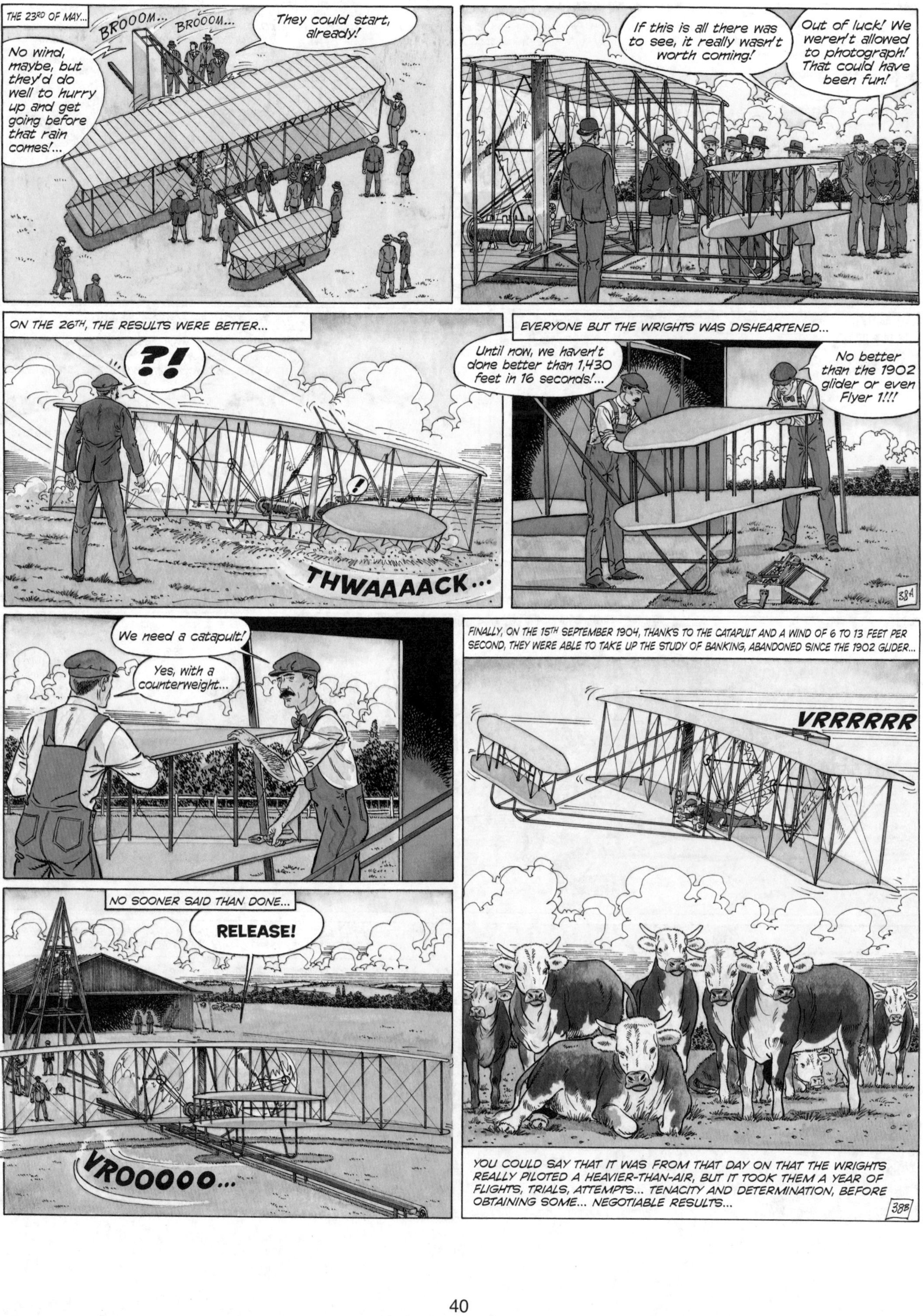
THE 23RD OF MAY...
BROOOM... BROOOM...
No wind, maybe, but they'd do well to hurry up and get going before that rain comes!...
They could start, already!
If this is all there was to see, it really wasn't worth coming!
Out of luck! We weren't allowed to photograph! That could have been fun!
ON THE 26TH, THE RESULTS WERE BETTER...
?!
!
THWAAAACK...
EVERYONE BUT THE WRIGHTS WAS DISHEARTENED...
Until now, we haven't done better than 1,430 feet in 16 seconds!...
No better than the 1902 glider or even Flyer 1!!!
We need a catapult!
Yes, with a counterweight...
NO SOONER SAID THAN DONE...
RELEASE!
VROOOOO...
FINALLY, ON THE 15TH SEPTEMBER 1904, THANKS TO THE CATAPULT AND A WIND OF 6 TO 13 FEET PER SECOND, THEY WERE ABLE TO TAKE UP THE STUDY OF BANKING, ABANDONED SINCE THE 1902 GLIDER...
VRRRRRR
YOU COULD SAY THAT IT WAS FROM THAT DAY ON THAT THE WRIGHTS REALLY PILOTED A HEAVIER-THAN-AIR, BUT IT TOOK THEM A YEAR OF FLIGHTS, TRIALS, ATTEMPTS... TENACITY AND DETERMINATION, BEFORE OBTAINING SOME... NEGOTIABLE RESULTS...

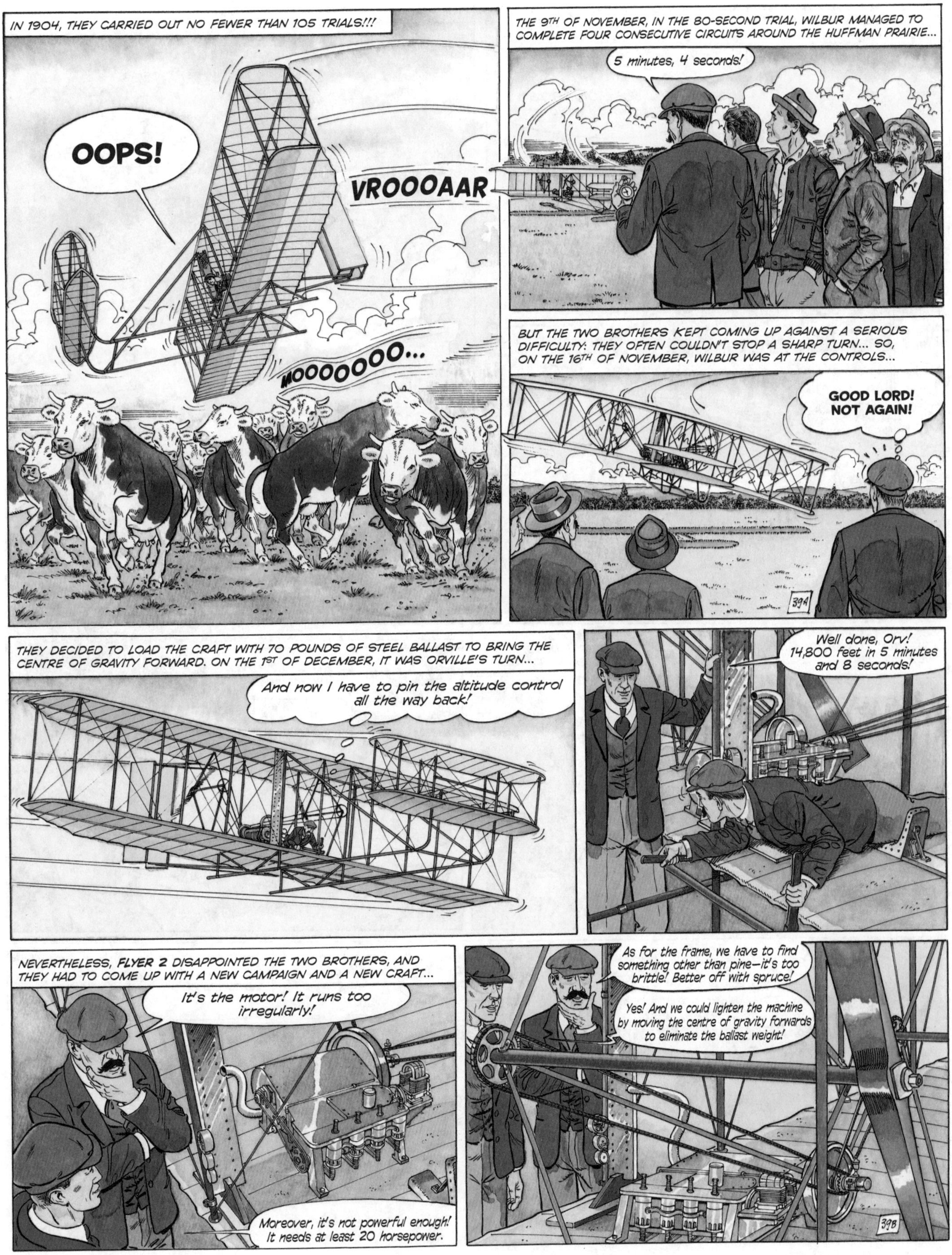

IN 1904, THEY CARRIED OUT NO FEWER THAN 105 TRIALS!!!
OOPS!
VROOOAAR
MOOOOOOO...
THE 9TH OF NOVEMBER, IN THE 80-SECOND TRIAL, WILBUR MANAGED TO COMPLETE FOUR CONSECUTIVE CIRCUITS AROUND THE HUFFMAN PRAIRIE...
5 minutes, 4 seconds!
BUT THE TWO BROTHERS KEPT COMING UP AGAINST A SERIOUS DIFFICULTY: THEY OFTEN COULDN'T STOP A SHARP TURN... SO, ON THE 16TH OF NOVEMBER, WILBUR WAS AT THE CONTROLS...
GOOD LORD! NOT AGAIN!
THEY DECIDED TO LOAD THE CRAFT WITH 70 POUNDS OF STEEL BALLAST TO BRING THE CENTRE OF GRAVITY FORWARD. ON THE 1ST OF DECEMBER, IT WAS ORVILLE'S TURN...
And now I have to pin the altitude control all the way back!
Well done, Orv! 14,800 feet in 5 minutes and 8 seconds!
NEVERTHELESS, FLYER 2 DISAPPOINTED THE TWO BROTHERS, AND THEY HAD TO COME UP WITH A NEW CAMPAIGN AND A NEW CRAFT...
It's the motor! It runs too irregularly!
Moreover, it's not powerful enough! It needs at least 20 horsepower.
As for the frame, we have to find something other than pine—it's too brittle! Better off with spruce!
Yes! And we could lighten the machine by moving the centre of gravity forwards to eliminate the ballast weight!

AND SO FLYER 3 WAS BORN, WITH WHICH THE TWO BROTHERS WOULD ACHIEVE SOME VERY CONVINCING PERFORMANCES... THE 4TH OF OCTOBER 1905...

Well done, Orv! 36.60 yards in 34 minutes!

THE NEXT DAY, WILBUR COVERED NEARLY 25 MILES...

BRROOOOO

BUT THE WRIGHT BROTHERS, NOW CONVINCED OF THEIR LEAD ON THE POTENTIAL COMPETITION, WOULD MAKE A SERIOUS ERROR: INDEED, THEY WOULDN'T FLY AGAIN UNTIL THE 8TH OF AUGUST, 1908, IN FRANCE...

No need to fly anymore now!

We should only take care of protecting our results from now on!...

And selling our machine!

... THEY TRIED, AND BY THE END OF 1905...

It's from the War Department...

And.?

Negative!

I've read the paper! There's a risk of war in Europe... If it doesn't work here, we could always offer it to another government for wartime use...

Absolutely! I have replied to this French captain who I'd told of our performances.

Yes, Captain Ferber...

He told me that his War Ministry might be interested...

And I offered it to him for... a million francs... only... payable after a demonstration of a 30-mile run...

THE FRENCH MINISTER IMMEDIATELY DISPATCHED AN EMISSARY TO NEGOTIATE THE PRICE, BUT...

600,000 FRANCS? Don't even think about it, Commandant Bonel! No!!!

LATER...

It's impossible for us to look after our own interests! That's not our area... We'd be better off asking a professional... Say, that one we contacted at Thanksgiving...

Yes, why not? Okay! Let's go with Charles Flint...*

*CHARLES RANLETT FLINT, THE "KING OF RUBBER," ALSO NICKNAMED THE "FATHER OF TRUSTS"

HART O. BERG*, CHARLES FLINT'S EUROPEAN REPRESENTATIVE, SOON BECAME QUITE ENTHUSIASTIC ABOUT THIS CAUSE, AND IT WAS HE WHO ORGANIZED AND FINANCED THE TWO BROTHERS' TRIP TO EUROPE... WILBUR LEFT FIRST...

*HART O. BERG, AN AMERICAN ENGINEER TRAINED AT THE UNIVERSITY OF LIEGE, SPECIALIST IN AUTOMATIC ARMS AT COLT, BUILDER OF TWO SUBMARINES AT SAINT PETERSBURG, RECRUITER OF FRENCH PILOTS FOR THE FIRST MEETING IN NEW YORK, INVENTOR OF, AMONGST OTHER THINGS, THE CARTON FOR LIQUID FOODS...

IN 1907, STILL IN DAYTON, ORVILLE BUILT *FLYER 4*, EQUIPPED WITH TWO SEATS. HE HAD IT PACKED INTO CASES AND SENT TO FRANCE, WHERE HE MET WILBUR.

In France, Captain Ferber is your most ardent supporter.

IN PARIS, LONG NEGOTIATIONS ENSUED...

BERG ALSO INTRODUCED THEM TO THE FRENCH MANUFACTURER BARIQUAND, WHO WOULD SUPPLY THE ENGINES FOR THEIR FUTURE PLANES.

What you need, gentlemen, is an engine with at least 20 horsepower!

BUT, FACED WITH THE COMPLEXITY OF THE NEGOTIATIONS, THE TWO BROTHERS PREFERRED TO MAKE WAY FOR THE PROFESSIONALS...

We're back in the United States, but we'll carry out the demonstration of our airplane in the spring of 1908 at the latest...

In order to sell it to the highest bidder!

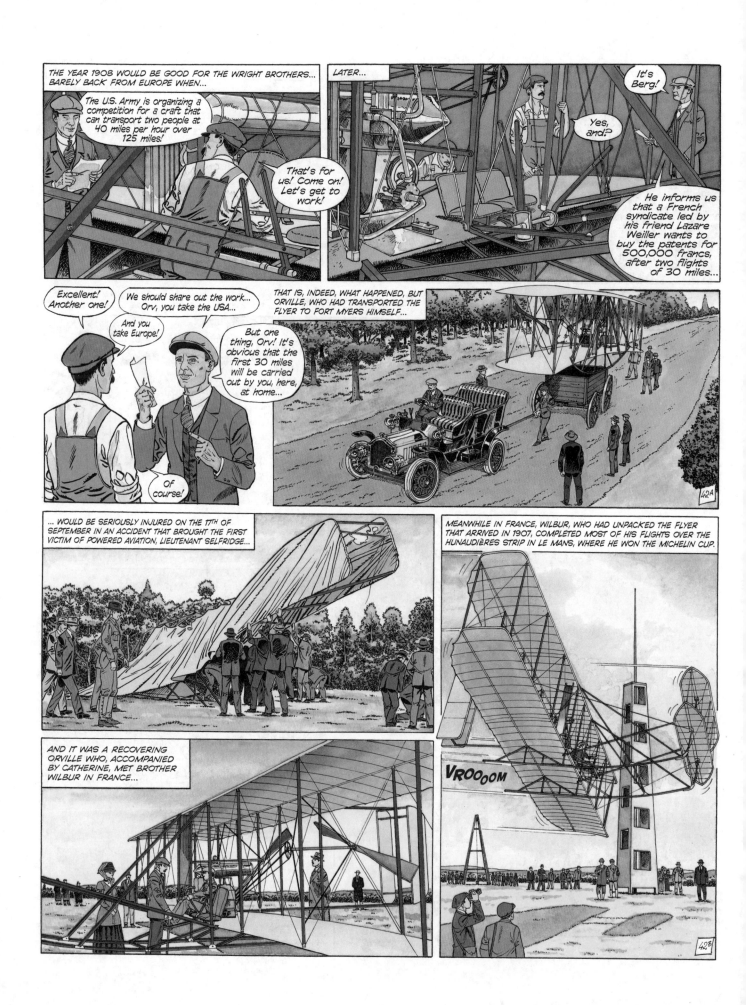

THE YEAR 1908 WOULD BE GOOD FOR THE WRIGHT BROTHERS... BARELY BACK FROM EUROPE WHEN...

The U.S. Army is organizing a competition for a craft that can transport two people at 40 miles per hour over 125 miles!

That's for us! Come on! Let's get to work!

LATER...

It's Berg!

Yes, and?

He informs us that a French syndicate led by his friend Lazare Weiller wants to buy the patents for 500,000 francs, after two flights of 30 miles...

Excellent! Another one!

We should share out the work... Orv, you take the USA...

And you take Europe!

But one thing, Orv! It's obvious that the first 30 miles will be carried out by you, here, at home...

Of course!

THAT IS, INDEED, WHAT HAPPENED, BUT ORVILLE, WHO HAD TRANSPORTED THE FLYER TO FORT MYERS HIMSELF...

... WOULD BE SERIOUSLY INJURED ON THE 17TH OF SEPTEMBER IN AN ACCIDENT THAT BROUGHT THE FIRST VICTIM OF POWERED AVIATION, LIEUTENANT SELFRIDGE...

AND IT WAS A RECOVERING ORVILLE WHO, ACCOMPANIED BY CATHERINE, MET BROTHER WILBUR IN FRANCE...

MEANWHILE IN FRANCE, WILBUR, WHO HAD UNPACKED THE FLYER THAT ARRIVED IN 1907, COMPLETED MOST OF HIS FLIGHTS OVER THE HUNAUDIÈRES STRIP IN LE MANS, WHERE HE WON THE MICHELIN CUP.

VROOOOM

WILBUR SET UP HIS OWN PILOTING SCHOOL AT PAU. HE WOULD TRAIN CIVIL AND MILITARY PILOTS THERE.

THEIR HOMECOMING WAS TRIUMPHANT. AFTER THEIR RECEPTION BY PRESIDENT TAFT, DAYTON WAS DRAPED IN FLAGS TO HONOUR THEM.

THE WRIGHTS ALSO WENT TO PRESENT THEIR AIRCRAFT IN ITALY AND GERMANY, BUT THEIR MAIN EUROPEAN SUCCESS WOULD BE THE MANUFACTURE, IN FRANCE, OF FLYERS BY THE FIRM ASTRA...

AND, AFTER THEY SOLEMNLY RECEIVED THE GOLDEN MEDAL OF CONGRESS, THEIR FATHER READ A PRAYER.

BUT THEY THEN WENT ON TO LAUNCH A SERIES OF COURT CASES IN THE UNITED STATES, FRANCE, GERMANY AND ENGLAND AGAINST ALL THOSE THEY SUSPECTED OF HAVING COPIED THEIR SYSTEM OF WARPING...

We have to drag this Curtiss into court!

Let's not forget Blériot, Farman, Voisin, Esnault-Pelterie, and the others...

IN ORDER TO SATISFY THE ORDERS OF THE AMERICAN ARMY, IN 1910 THEY CREATED THE WRIGHT COMPANY WITH A FACTORY IN DAYTON...

BUT ALREADY, IN AUGUST 1909, AT THE REIMS MEETING...

This Curtiss is incredible! He's even beaten Blériot!

Of course! He'll put the Wrights to shame!

AND IN NOVEMBER THE FOLLOWING YEAR, AT THE BELMONT PARK MEETING IN NEW YORK, THE TWO MAIN RIVALS FOR THE LIBERTY PRIZE WERE... BLÉRIOTS!

SO IT WAS THE AMERICAN JOHN MOISANT WHO WON THE LIBERTY RACE, AND THE WRIGHT BROTHERS, WHO MADE ONE OF THEIR LAST PUBLIC APPEARANCES THERE, JOINED IN THE CELEBRATIONS...

WILBUR WOULD SUCCUMB TO TYPHOID FEVER* TWO YEARS LATER. ORVILLE SOLD THE COMPANY IN 1915 AND IT LATER WENT ON TO BECOME WHAT IS KNOWN TODAY AS THE CURTISS-WRIGHT CORPORATION.

*MILTON WOULD DIE IN 1917 AND ORVILLE IN 1948.

AS FOR THE BIPLANE FORMULA, WHICH TRIUMPHED THROUGHOUT THE FIRST WORLD WAR, IT WAS SOON REPLACED BY THE MONOPLANE, EXEMPLIFIED BY THE BLÉRIOT XI, A REAL PIONEER IN THIS AREA.

BLÉRIOT XI (1909)

BUT EVERYONE KNOWS, AND NOBODY TODAY CONTESTS, THE FACT THAT THE WRIGHT BROTHERS WERE THE FIRST IN THE WORLD, IN THE HISTORY OF AVIATION, TO PUSH THE AIRPLANE TO PERFECTION AS FAR AS ALLOWING IT TO GLIDE WITH EASE UNDER THE CONTROL OF A PILOT. (PIERRE LISSARAGUE).

LOCHEED F22 RAPTOR

SUPERMARINE SPITFIRE (1938)

THE END

- MARCEL UDERZO + JEAN-PIERRE LEFÈVRE-GARROS -

Cinebook recounts
A Collection of Real History Books

Battle of Britain

We need pilots... We've drawn from our volunteers in France, Belgium, Poland, Czechoslovakia and elsewhere. These "amateurs" from the reserves have become veterans!

Have they lost their fun, eccentric side in the exchange?

NOT QUITE... THE RESERVE FORCES HAD BEEN BUILT UP SINCE 1925. MEMBERS OF THE AUXILIARY FORCES, VOLUNTEERS FOR THE RESERVES, UNIVERSITY AVIATION GROUPS, THESE "AMATEURS" HAD KEPT THEIR TASTE FOR TRICKERY. SO, AT THE START OF THE WAR, SQUADRON 611...

Look! They've formed a swastika!

Ha! I remember that story!

Coming back to the criticism of certain people, I would like to point out that I will not budge on this tactic, no more than I did to take from the North of England to help the South!

INDEED, THE 2ND OF AUGUST 1940, AT KARINHALL, GOERING'S RESIDENCE...

On the 30th of July, the Führer gave me the order for a total assault. It will take place around the 13th of August and will be called "Day of the Eagle." The success of our invasion will depend on this victory.

THE PLAN FOR THIS ATTACK WAS AS FOLLOWS:

LUFTFLOTTE V: STUMPAF
LUFTFLOTTE II: KESSERLING

FIGHTERS:
BOMBERS:
PARIS
STUKA
LUFTFLOTTE III: SPERRLE

ON THE 30TH OF JULY 1940, IN BERCHTESGADEN, ADMIRAL ROEDER HAD A FEW DOUBTS...

We need total air domination! Mine sweeping to prepare for the invasion will take five weeks. I'm not sure about a full and definitive victory over the R.A.F.!

THE FIRST PHASE OF THE BATTLE BEGAN ON THE 8TH OF AUGUST...

Cinebook recounts Vol. 1 - Battle of Britain

Cinebook recounts

A Collection of Real History Books

Cinebook recounts
The Falklands War

ON THE 18TH OF MARCH 1982, THE ARGENTINIANS TEST BRITISH REACTIONS AND SEND 40 "WORKERS" ONTO A DEMOLITION SITE IN SOUTH GEORGIA TO RAISE THE ARGENTINIAN FLAG. THE JUNTA IS REINFORCED IN ITS ATTEMPTS, INASMUCH AS THEY HAVE HEARD ABOUT THE WITHDRAWAL OF THE ENDURANCE.

IN LONDON...

Since his takeover in December 1981, General Galtieri has stated that the Argentine flag will fly over the Falklands before 1984... Now, our intelligence tells us that the Argentinians are preparing a strike...

Perhaps we should keep the Endurance out there?

... And consider sending a nuclear submarine?

Is their military activity very high?...

They say that they are preparing manoeuvres with the Uruguayan navy.

THE JUNTA MADE ITS DECISION. ADMIRAL ANAYA DECLARED: "... 17 YEARS OF NEGOTIATIONS, 148 YEARS OF WAITING, TOO MUCH!" TWO GROUPS OF ARGENTINE SHIPS ARE SENT SOUTH. ONE GROUP, MADE UP OF "DE MAYO," DESTROYERS "HERCULES," "SEGUI" AND "C.PY," AS WELL AS LANDING GEAR, HEADS TO THE FALKLANDS, WHILE THE OTHER, ARMED WITH CORVETTE MISSILE LAUNCHERS, MAKES ITS WAY TO SOUTH GEORGIA. THE ATTACK MUST TAKE PLACE ON THE NIGHT OF APRIL 1ST, 1982.

2